THE CHILDREN'S ANGER-CONTROL BOOK

DON'T RANT & RAVE ON WEDNESDAYS!

WRITTEN BY

ADOLPH MOSER
Ed.D.

ILLUSTRATED BY

DAVID MELTON

LANDMARK EDITIONS, INC.

1904 Foxridge Drive • Kansas City, KS 66106 • www.landmarkeditions.com

Dedicated to
Nancy,
who got it all started.

Tenth Printing

TEXT COPYRIGHT © 1994 BY ADOLPH J. MOSER, Ed.D.

ILLUSTRATIONS COPYRIGHT © 1994 BY DAVID MELTON

International Standard Book Number: 0-933849-54-0 (LIB.BDG.)

Library of Congress Cataloging-in-Publication Data
Moser, Adolph, 1938-
  Don't rant & rave on Wednesdays! : the children's anger-control book / written by
Adolph Moser ; illustrated by David Melton.
    p.   cm.
ISBN 0-933849-54-0 (lib.bdg.)
    1. Anger—Juvenile literature.
    2. Temper tantrums—Juvenile literature.   [1. Anger.]
I. Melton, David, 1934-   ill.   II. Title.
III. Title: Do not rant and rave on Wednesdays!
BF575.A5M67   1994   152.4'7—dc20   94-22775
                                                                  CIP
                                                                  AC

Editorial Coordinator: Nancy R. Thatch
Creative Coordinator: David Melton

Printed in the United States of America

Landmark Editions, Inc.
1904 Foxridge Drive
Kansas City, Kansas 66106
913-722-0700
www.landmarkeditions.com

Dear Friend:

When I was a boy, I often got very angry.

Some people told me to "let all my anger out."

So I didn't hesitate to yell and scream, shake my fists, and stomp my feet!

I let my anger out all right. But that kind of behavior got me into a lot of fights and arguments. It also got me into trouble at school and at home.

Now that I am an adult, I still get angry. But I don't get as angry as often as I used to, and I don't stay angry as long. I have learned how to control my behavior when I'm angry. I no longer get into fights, and I don't get into as many arguments. I get along much better with other people, and I stay out of trouble. That makes me a much happier person.

It is important that you understand your own anger and learn how to deal with it in positive ways. So I wrote this book just for you.

— Your Friend,
Adolph Moser

P.S. If you know some other RANTERS and RAVERS, you might want to share this book with them.

It happens every day —
some people get so upset!

They shake their fists,
they stomp their feet,

they jump up and down,
and they RANT and RAVE!

Sometimes —
they call people bad names,

throw things across the room,
and break everything they can.

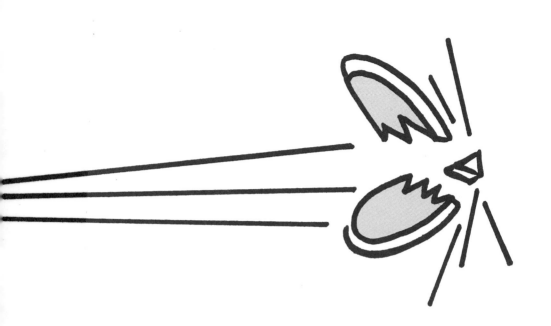

Some people do
all of those things,
and even more,
when they are ANGRY!

9

Anger is the
upset feeling we have
when we become
very annoyed
or really mad.

Anger affects our thinking,
excites our emotions,
and makes our muscles become tense.

Everyone becomes angry
now and then —
young people, old people,
tall people, short people,

fat people, thin people,
nice people, mean people
men people, women people,
boy people and girl people —

Everyone!
Including you!

People can become angry
quicker and easier
when they don't feel well
or when they are
in a grumpy mood.

Some adults become angry as many as twelve times every day.

Children
can become angry
that often, too...
and so can you!

You can become angry
about things
other people say or do —
   Someone calls you a bad name
   or makes fun of you.

Or someone pushes you
or hits you,

or breaks your favorite toy.

You can also become angry
over things that happen —

You stub your toe
or bump your head.

You spill grape juice
on your best shirt.

Or you dent your new bicycle

Or you lose your lunch money
or forget your homework.

When people are angry,
they may say funny things
and do funny things.

But they don't like for
anyone to laugh at them.

When people are angry,
they may yell at others.
But they don't want others
to yell back at them.

If anyone laughs
or yells at them,
they may become even angrier.

When angry people
become even angrier,
they may lose control
of their actions.
They may hit other people,

When you see people
who are extremely angry,
it is best to
stay out of their way
until they calm down.

When some people get angry,
they don't RANT and RAVE
in front of anyone.

They hide their anger
deep down inside,
and they don't tell anyone
that they are upset.

People should not hold
too much anger inside.
That can make them
become angrier and angrier.
It can also make them sick.

It is okay
for you to feel angry
and tell others
how you feel.

But it is not all right
for you to hit people
or break things.

Some people think
anger is bad,
but that is not true.
Anger is a feeling,
and feelings are
neither good nor bad.

ANGER

It is how you BEHAVE
when you feel angry
that can be either good or bad.

As people grow older,
they are expected
to have better control
of their BEHAVIOR,
even when they are angry.

If we see
a small child
having a temper tantrum,

we might
think his BEHAVIOR is cute
or even funny.

29

But we wouldn't think
it was funny if we saw
the president of the United States
on national television,
and he was jumping up and down,
yelling and screaming,
and beating his fists
against a podium.

We would probably say:
"Even if the president is angry,
he should be able
to control his BEHAVIOR
better than that!"

Feeling too much anger
or becoming angry too often
can be harmful to us.

Doctors find that people
who are not able
to control their
RANTING and RAVING
have more arguments
and get into more fights.
They are more apt to lie and steal,
cut classes and drop out of school.
They become sick more often,
and they are more likely
to become involved with drugs.

When other people —
> your mother, your father,
> your sister, your brother,
> your friends, or your teachers
> RANT and RAVE,
> don't blame yourself.
> You are not responsible
> for their anger.

They are responsible for
dealing with their own anger
and controlling their own behavior.

And other people are not
responsible for your anger
or your behavior.

YOU are responsible for
dealing with your own anger
and controlling your own behavior.

We human beings
can quickly change
from feeling calm and friendly
to feeling mad and furious
because...

we have a super-fast
communication system between
our THOUGHTS,
our EMOTIONS, and
our TENSIONS.

That super-fast system works like this —
When someone or something bothers you,
you immediately have the THOUGHT,
   "I don't like that!"

And zap! Faster than greased lightning,
that THOUGHT is sent
to your EMOTIONS!

Your EMOTIONS become excited,
and they send a flash alert
to your muscles.

Your muscles build up with TENSIONS,

and in a split second,
you are ready
TO THROW A FIT
OR START A FIGHT!

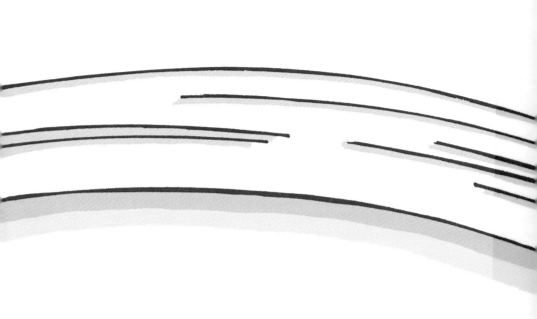

When you are very angry,
it is difficult for you
to think clearly.

When you can't think clearly,
your EMOTIONS and your TENSIONS
can race out of control.

And that is like
speeding down the highway
at one hundred miles per hour,
in a car that has
NO STEERING WHEEL!

Before you race out of control,
Put on the BRAKES!
And STOP whatever you are doing!

Give yourself
time to calm down by
COUNTING TO TEN SLOWLY —

1-2-3-4-5-6-7-8-9-10

If you still feel upset,
keep on counting to —

30...40...50...100

By staying calm,
you will be able to
think more clearly.

And you will have
a better chance
to LISTEN to what
your THOUGHTS are telling you.

The calmer you remain,
the less angry you will become.
The less angry you become,
the better you
can control your BEHAVIOR.

If you want to develop
more control over your own behavior
and learn how to deal with your anger,
you can do that.

Select a day
when you would like to begin.
How about next Wednesday?

Make a sign that reads —

And hang that sign in your room.

Then...
first thing on Wednesday morning,
look at the sign.

DON'T
RANT and RAVE
ON
WEDNESDAYS
!

Remember what the sign says
all day long.

And no matter what happens
on Wednesday,
  DON'T RANT AND RAVE!
    Instead — STOP!
        COUNT TO TEN,

    or even to ONE HUNDRED.
    While you count,
    STAY CALM
    and LISTEN TO YOUR THOUGHTS.

49

To calm yourself even more,
try to think about something else —
     Watch a funny show on television
     or read a book of jokes.

Laughing will make you feel better,
because when you laugh,
your brain makes chemicals
that produce pain killers.

When you are angry
and your muscles are loaded
with extra energy,

instead of RANTING and RAVING,
put that energy to good use —
   Clean your room.
   Wash the dishes.
   Straighten your closet.
As you use this energy,
you will begin to calm down.

WALK your anger away.
When you become so angry
that you want to RANT and RAVE,
just turn and WALK AWAY —

WALK to your room.
WALK outside.
WALK around the block.
WALK long enough to reduce
the amount of anger you feel.

Hitting a punching bag,
or playing football,
or doing other violent activities
may not reduce your anger.

Violent activities
can often increase
your level of anger.

Tell someone how you feel —
   TALK to a friend,
   or your parents,
   or to one of your teachers.

And listen to their suggestions.
Then calmly decide
what you think you should do.

54

TALK yourself out of ANGER.
Yes, you can do that.

TALK to yourself the same way
you would talk to an upset friend.
Just say to yourself —
"Now, don't be so angry.
This isn't so bad.
Stay calm and relax.
Don't get so mad."

WRITE or DRAW your anger away —
Write down the things you feel
or draw a picture of them.

As you write or draw,
imagine that your anger
is flowing out through the pencil
and onto the paper.

BATHE your anger away.
Fill the bathtub with warm water
and lie down in it.

Imagine your anger is leaving your body
and melting away in the warm water
that surrounds you.

Learning how to
deal with your anger
takes practice.

The more you practice,
the better you will become.

As you become better
at dealing with your anger,
you will find that
you don't get angry as often.

And you will gain
more and more control
of your behavior.

Anytime you have
successfully
reduced your anger
and controlled your behavior —

CONGRATULATE YOURSELF!
Give yourself a pat on the back
and say to yourself —
"Good job! Well done!"

If you can go all day
on Wednesday
without RANTING and RAVING,
then you can do the same
on Thursday, and Friday,
and EVERY DAY of the week,
and on EVERY DAY
for the rest of your life!

YOU CAN DO IT!

EMOTIONAL IMPACT SERIES

Children love these books because they help children deal with real problems that they face every day.

Counselors, teachers, and parents appreciate the practical advice these books offer to the youngsters who are in their care.

These Outstanding Books Are Highly Recommended

Much-needed books!
I enthusiastically recommend all of them to parents, teachers, clinicians, and, of course, to children.
— Theodore Tollefson, Ph.D. Clinical Psychologist

Delightful and practical!
You don't have to be a psychologist to read these books to a child. Better still, have a child read them to you.
— Larry M. Hubble, Ph.D. Psychologist

What helpful books for teaching children important methods of self-control. I highly recommend them!
— Suzanne Leiphant, Ph.D. Clinical Psychologist & Author

Informative, compassionate, wise!
These helpful handbooks clearly explain and entertain at the same time.
— Dr. Taylor McGee, HSPP Child Psychologist

One only has to read today's headlines or hear the news to realize how much these books are needed.
— Phyllis Morrison Grateful Parent

These are very important books.
I have no doubt they could help save the lives of many children and adults, too.
— R.M. Fortrell, Ph.D. Psychologist

SEVEN BOOKS! SEVEN DAYS!

STRESS!

ISBN 0-933849-18-4

SELF-ESTEEM!

ISBN 0-933849-38-9

ANGER!

ISBN 0-933849-54-0

GRIEF!

ISBN 0-933849-60-5

TRUTH!

ISBN 0-933849-76-1

DIVORCE!

ISBN 0-933849-77-X

VIOLENCE!

ISBN 0-933849-79-6

ALL SEVEN ARE IMPORTANT BOOKS!

In these very informative and highly
entertaining handbooks for children,
Dr. Adolph Moser offers practical approaches
and effective techniques to help youngsters
deal with the problems of –

*STRESS, SELF-ESTEEM, ANGER, GRIEF,
TRUTH, DIVORCE,* and *VIOLENCE.*

The colorful illustrations created by artists
Dav Pilkey and David Melton project
perfect blends of humor and sensitivity.

YOU'LL WANT ALL OF THEM!

Adolph Moser — author

Dr. Adolph Moser is a licensed clinical psychologist in private practice, specializing in bio-behavioral and cognitive approaches to stress-related syndromes. He is founder of the Center for Human Potential, a nonprofit organization with holistic focus on preventing acute onsets of stress in children. While Chief Psychologist at the Indiana Youth Center, he implemented a biofeedback laboratory and directed a nine-year research project on the effects of relaxation techniques in the treatment of stress disorders. That study culminated in the development of the nationally distributed stress-management program, entitled SYSTEMATIC RELAXATION TRAINING.

Raised in Indiana, Dr. Moser is a graduate of the universities of Purdue and Indiana. He is certified in biofeedback and is a Diplomate Stressologist. He is also a Diplomate in Behavioral Medicine and Psychotherapy, and a Fellow and Diplomate in Medical Psychotherapy. Dr. Moser is listed in WHO'S WHO IN THE BIO-BEHAVIORAL SCIENCES. In 1987, he received the "Outstanding Psychologist of the Year" award from the National Prisoners' Rights Union.

After becoming parents, Dr. Moser and his then wife expanded their professional practices to include normal problems of childhood and parenting. They co-authored a newspaper column, "Positive Parenting," for ten years.

Dr. Moser is the divorced father of two grown children and one adolescent, which explains his perennial interest in stress and anger management.

All of Dr. Moser's books in his EMOTIONAL IMPACT SERIES have received outstanding reviews and enthusiastic acceptance from children, parents, counselors, and educators nationwide.

David Melton — illustrator

David Melton was one of the most versatile and prolific talents on the modern literary and art scenes. His literary works spanned the gamut of factual prose, analytical essays, newsreporting, magazine articles, features, short stories, and poetry and novels in both the adult and juvenile fields. Since 1968, he had thirty-two books published. Several were translated into a number of languages.

Mr. Melton illustrated ten of his own books and six by other authors. Many of his drawings and paintings were reproduced as fine art prints, posters, puzzles, calendars, book jackets, record covers, mobiles, and note cards, and have been featured in national publications.

Since a number of Mr. Melton's books were and still are enjoyed by children, he was a frequent visitor to hundreds of schools throughout the country as a principal speaker in Author-in-Residence Programs, Young Authors' Days, and Children's Literature Festivals. He also conducted his WRITTEN & ILLUSTRATED BY... workshops for students and educators which effectively taught participants to write and illustrate their own original books.

Mr. Melton's highly-acclaimed teacher's manual, WRITTEN & ILLUSTRATED BY..., is used by thousands of teachers nationwide to instruct their students how to write and illustrate amazing books. In 1986, Mr. Melton initiated the annual NATIONAL WRITTEN & ILLUSTRATED BY... CONTEST FOR STUDENTS. This annual competition provided an opportunity for students' works to be professionally published.

David Melton passed away in November of 2002.